The Legend of Saint Alban

by

John Lydgate

In a Modern English Prose Version

by Simon Webb

Published by the Langley Press, Durham, 2016

The cover shows a detail of The Martyrdom of St Alban from British Library Manuscript Royal 2 B VI
(St Albans c. 1246-c. 1260)

Also from the Langley Press:

In Search of Saint Alban

Nicholas Breakspear: The Pope from England

In Search of Bede

In Search of the Northern Saints

The Legend of Saint Cuthbert

The Valentine's Day Book

Chaucer's *Parliament of Fowls*
in a Modern English Verse Translation

For free downloads and more from the Langley Press, visit our
website at: http://tinyurl.com/lpdirect

Contents

John Lydgate: from a nineteenth-century print

Introduction

A fifteenth-century bookworm transported forward in time to the twenty-first century would no doubt be surprised by many things. Among these would be the fact that few people in our century have heard of our time-traveller's contemporary, the poet John Lydgate.

Lydgate was regarded, during his own lifetime (and for a long time afterwards) as one of the greatest of the English poets; a writer comparable in stature to Geoffrey Chaucer. Lydgate was heavily influenced by Chaucer, used a rhyme-scheme named for Chaucer, and was even a friend of the poet's son Thomas.

One reason why Lydgate's poetry is neglected today may have to do with its religious content. As well as being a prolific poet, Lydgate was also a religious one, which is hardly surprising given his status as a monk of Bury St Edmunds. Religious poetry has an uncertain status among modern readers, particularly in England. In modern poetry, religious feeling is often expressed in terms of a vague general spirituality, rather than in the forthright Church-Christian terminology of Lydgate and his contemporaries.

Parts of Lydgate's poem on Saint Alban are obviously written to reinforce the Christian message as it existed in the minds of the poet's readers, and his *hearers* if we assume that the poem or parts of it were read aloud in church, as were other saints' lives. The variety of Christianity presented to us in his

St Alban has many characteristics that indicate its medieval Roman Catholic origins – these include the emphasis on such things as the Trinity, the Incarnation of Christ and the role of the Virgin Mary.

John Lydgate's narrative poem the *Life of St Albon and St Amphabell*, which I have re-named *The Legend of St Alban* for this edition, was written in 1439. It was a commission for Lydgate from John Whethamstede, the abbot of St Albans. The abbot, who was also known as John Bostock, was an ambitious man and a close friend of Humphrey, Duke of Gloucester, once a protector of the realm during the minority of King Henry VI, and a man who features in Shakespeare's plays about that unfortunate king. Humphrey was only one of the very distinguished people of the time who acted as patrons to the poet John Lydgate. This impressive list also included two English kings: Henry V and his son, the aforementioned Henry VI.

Lydgate had written a long narrative poem called *The Lives of Saints Edmund and Fremund* six years before he wrote his Alban poem, and it would seem that it was this earlier work that inspired Whethamstede to commission Lydgate to write a similar narrative about his own local saint. Lydgate was paid £3 6s. 8d. for completion of this work, a magnificent manuscript of which was placed before the altar at St Albans.

The poem runs to over thirty-five thousand words in its entirety, which contrasts with the earlier, much more authoritative account of Alban given by Bede, the Anglo-Saxon monk and scholar: in English translation, Bede's version comes to less than sixteen *hundred* words.

Lydgate no doubt wanted to give John Whethamstede, the commissioner of the poem, something substantial in return for his fee, which would be worth over fifteen hundred pounds today. But it is unlikely that the poet wrote at such length just to satisfy his patron. Alban was martyred over a thousand years before Lydgate set quill to parchment, and Bede's brief account of the martyrdom of the saint was already over seven hundred years old in Lydgate's day; it is, therefore, hardly surprising if extra details had accumulated around Alban's story by the time Lydgate got to it. The poet may have felt compelled to include these details, so as not to disappoint his readers, for whom the additions may have been central to their idea of the saint.

Whether they are Lydgate's additions, or come from earlier authors, or the oral tradition, the elaborations sewn onto Alban's myth may have been welcomed in medieval times because of the high status of the saint in question, and the importance accorded to the city outside which he was martyred.

Lydgate calls Alban 'protomartyr of England', and the saint's position as the first recorded saint to have perished in what is now called England remains unchallenged. He seems to have been well-established as an important local saint by the time the city of St Albans was visited by the French bishop St Germanus around 480 AD. Alban's cult also received a major boost near the end of the eighth century, when the Anglo-Saxon king Offa 'discovered' the saint's body. Another boost came in the twelfth century, when local boy Nicholas Breakspear became pope. During the Englishman's pontificate, the privileges of the church institutions connected to St Albans were confirmed and enlarged. Thanks to the city's religious prestige, the abbot of St Albans took precedence over the other 'mitred' abbots when a national parliament was called. This high status also had financial benefits: at the time of the Dissolution of the Monasteries, the annual income of the church of St Albans was worth the equivalent of over half a million pounds in modern money.

Lydgate and others may have felt instinctively that, though the foundation of the Alban myth was strong in itself, it really needed to be enlarged if it was to be adequate to support the overgrown edifice that was Alban's medieval importance and reputation. When the building is enlarged, after all, it is always wise to consider enlarging the foundations as well.

How, then, did Lydgate manage to stretch his material so that it became over twenty times its original length?

Only a relatively small section in the middle of Lydgate's poem relates to Alban's conversion to Christianity, and his subsequent martyrdom. After he has killed off Alban, the poet goes on to the subsequent life and death of Alban's fellow-saint Amphibalus. Earlier in the poem, before Alban even meets Amphibalus, the man who converts him to Christianity, Lydgate treats us to a lengthy relation of what Hollywood film-makers would call Alban's 'back-story'. This amounts to the equivalent of a Hollywood 'prequel'; not answering the question 'what happened next', but rather, 'what happened before'. This prequel includes details of how Alban and Amphibalus were acquainted before the latter arrived in Verulamium, the city that became St Albans.

In fact there is much of the Hollywood screen-writer, or even novelist, in Lydgate. As often happens with later versions of myths and legends, whether Christian or otherwise, Lydgate answers many of the questions that remain unanswered by the shorter initial narrative.

Bede does not really tell us who Alban was: Lydgate asserts that he was a handsome young nobleman; an important man in the Roman city of Verulamium, and indeed in Britain as a whole, who used to go about in a cloak fringed with gold. In

Bede's account, it is unclear what the locals of Verulamium think of the persecution of Alban, which is blamed entirely on the Roman emperor, the local judge, and some of his agents. All Bede's townspeople do is turn out in large numbers to witness Alban's execution outside the city walls. Lydgate, by contrast, is convinced that most if not all of the inhabitants of the Roman city are almost insane with blood-lust against Alban and Amphibalus.

Lydgate is going beyond his most reliable sources in giving Alban's mentor and fellow-saint a name. The name 'Amphibalus' is derived from the Greek name for a type of cloak that the saint might have worn: Amphibalus is therefore 'St Cloak'. The poet also names the judge or magistrate who leads the persecution of Alban: here he is 'Asclepiodotus', a name that shows how Lydgate tries to make his story more real by linking it to other historical events and personalities his readers might recognise as being part of his period. Julius Asclepiodotus was a real Roman prefect who served under the emperor Diocletian. Maximian, nick-named Hercules, whom Lydgate also introduces into his story, was co-emperor with Diocletian, a notorious persecutor of Christians. Modern historians assert that it is unclear whether Alban's murder could have happened during Diocletian's time: Lydgate seems entirely confident that it did.

Lydgate not only makes bold to answer the questions raised by shorter accounts of his story: he also tries to make the story more believable by adding, in the words of W.S. Gilbert, 'corroborative detail, intended to give artistic verisimilitude to an otherwise bald and unconvincing narrative'. One way Lydgate does this is by smoothing out the most obvious wrinkle in the story: the question of how Alban could have become such a devout and self-sacrificing Christian after only

11

a brief acquaintance with the religion? Lydgate tries to solve this problem in the narrative by giving Alban a vivid dream or vision during which he sees the central events of the life of Jesus as if at first hand. The poet also introduces a pause of at least six weeks between Alban's rapid conversion and his martyrdom.

As well as adding a lot of extra detail to the original story, Lydgate gives it a distinctly medieval flavour, so that sometimes we feel we are reading a story set in a city in fifteenth-century France, rather than a tale of Roman Britain. This sort of thing is familiar to readers of Chaucer, whose poem *Troilus and Criseyde*, for instance, is supposed to be set in ancient Troy, but is closer in atmosphere to the court of King Richard II of England. In Lydgate's St Alban poem, both Alban and Amphibalus are knights in the best medieval style, dubbed by the same emperor whose persecutions did for both of them in the end. Lydgate also tells us that, though his hero may be naked and unarmed as he faces his persecutors, Alban is protected by his faith in a way that is entirely consistent with medieval knighthood. This verse from Lydgate's original hammers the point home, and reminds the reader how many obscure pieces of ironmongery went to make up a medieval suit of armour:

His sabbatons set on grounde of trouthe,
And his greues forged with stabilnes.
And his polayns plyant without slouthe,
And his quisshews borne vp with high prowesse,
A payre of curesse / closed with ryghtwysenesse,
And his vauntbrace was truste that went beforne,
Rerebrace of charyte / which myght not be forlorne . . .

The modern English prose adaptation printed below covers the crucial middle section of Lydgate's poem, which itself comprises the poet's elaborated version of the basic Alban legend as re-told by Bede. Although I have selected only a small part of the original, I have still found it necessary to cut out some verses, and sections of verses, where Lydgate repeats himself, contradicts himself, goes off at a tangent, or goes into so much detail that the thread of the story is in danger of becoming lost.

The verse printed above, which is not reflected in my adaptation, is a case in point. Having established the idea that Alban is 'naked', perhaps meaning that he is unarmed, but that his arms and armour are faith, hope, etc., the poet prolongs this idea over three verses, where he introduces a catalogue of the things a knight would typically need in battle: everything from weapons and specific pieces of armour to 'counsayle' (counsel or advice) and a 'guyde' (meaning a guide or scout, needed in medieval warfare because whole armies would regularly lose their way, failing to find the enemy they were supposed to engage, or the castle they were supposed to besiege).

Lydgate's enumeration of the different pieces of medieval armour in this context shows that, as is also demonstrated by his introduction into the story of the values of medieval knighthood, Lydgate is not concerned to give us a truly 'antiqued' picture of Roman Verulamium, as a modern novelist tackling this subject surely would. Like the painters and sculptors of his period, Lydgate clothes his characters in what to him would have been modern dress.

Another medieval, and indeed Chaucerian, aspect of Lydgate's poem is his tendency to introduce pagan deities into descriptions of natural phenomena. When the natural world dries up in response to Alban's ill-treatment, Flora, Phoebus and Aeolus are invoked; and earlier in the poem Amphibalus himself refers to Phoebus during his description of the time of year when the Virgin Mary was visited by the Angel Gabriel. This technique shows that, like the best minds of his age, Lydgate's was able to contain both classical and Christian ideas; but the approach seems a little incongruous when Alban's pagan persecutors assert that they actually worship Phoebus, and even attribute the miracles surrounding Alban's death to the pagan sun-god.

The Legend of Saint Alban

The merits of St Alban are recognised by the Lord, as surely as Aurora parts the curtains of the night to let in Phoebus, and as surely as Lucifer brings news of a glad morning. Under the influence of heaven, everything follows its own nature, whether good or bad: virtuous people can prosper by perfect providence, if sensuality is bridled with reason.

The example of Tacitus shows us that people can live good lives even though they are pagans, as long as they are taught by nature. In the same way, wheat comes from chaff, and good comes out of evil, as is proved by the life of St Eustace. Who taught Trajan how to do the right thing, when he was confronted by the grieving widow? Despite all his power, the emperor made time for her, and reason taught him to behave righteously, and to redress her wrongs. The old stories tell us that this same Trajan avoided the eternal pains of hell's prison because St Gregory prayed for him. This shows us how God takes note of good deeds, and rewards every one of them.

But to return to my tale; during his time of great power the blessed Alban fostered truth and did no wrong to anyone. For this, the Lord did not fail to stretch out his finger and choose Alban as his knight, to be converted and turned to his Law. His truthfulness, his well-grounded virtue, his native gentleness, caused God of his merciful goodness to take this prince into his service, and to remove him from the worship of false idols. Alban became God's chosen champion, a new Titan, lit up by the rising sun!

(With God's help, I now intend to show how Alban followed righteousness, and ruled every part of his city with prudent policy.)

The Romans found it suited them to ordain Alban, by commission and imperial title, as prince and steward throughout all Britain. For his part, Alban took pains to avoid all trouble, and to rule the people in peace. He provided laws that were so mighty and so strong, and so carefully designed to ensure everyone's benefit, that no man wronged another man while Alban ruled. Where he saw innocents oppressed, he quickly took pains to redress their wrongs.

He made the rich live off their own wealth, without extorting money from the poor. He also repressed riotous behaviour and suffered no dissension. He forced idle people to work, and provided food for everyone, though nobody was allowed to eat and be lazy. Alban was loved and feared by people of high and low degree, and would not abandon truth for either friend or foe. Good people loved him for his goodness, the rich feared him, and he pitied the poor. He was not slow to right wrongs, and his judgements were as steadfast as a wall, lacking any partiality.

Nature and the law taught Alban to run away from all vices, and to be an enemy of all dishonesty. He never gave his judgement until the truth had been revealed, and then his sentences were neither too heavy nor too light. His disposition led him to make a judgement as the matter at hand dictated.

Alban was also acquainted with the four cardinal virtues: he rode Temperance like a horse, he was ruled by Merciful Righteousness, and defended Truth. His warlike manliness used force and skill to punish all falseness. He could appease people who wanted to make trouble, and calm all rancour wherever he saw it. Like a knightly prince, he hated liars, and stopped his ears to all flattery. He did not listen to quarrellers until he had seen all the parties involved for himself. He rigorously punished envious slander, which is made up of malice, hatred and defamation. He was always an enemy to those who spoke with a double tongue, who were not ashamed to speak evil of others all the time, and backbiters who never used their lips to speak well: young and old, this prince threw all such people out of his house.

He could tell when to punish and when to let be: his heart had no duplicity in it, and it proved itself to be a a big heart to people who went about naked under the sky; his gate was always open for hospitality. In fact, I haven't the cunning or the language to describe the virtues Alban possessed, even from a young age. But I will continue (and offer no excuse for so doing) to declare how God dealt with this knight, and I will describe how Amphibalus entered the city of Verulamium, and how he and Alban met.

Amphibalus entered the city, seeking bed and board. He went up and down the streets, looking like a pilgrim. Eventually he came across Alban, with a great multitude of people. The prince was proceeding in state through the city, in a garment fringed with gold. Amphibalus made bold to humbly beg him for hospitality.

Amphibalus recognised Alban after he had looked at him more closely. He remembered how, long years before, they had visited Rome together. For God's sake Amphibalus begged Alban to receive him into his own house: the story tells us that Alban was always granting hospitality to people of every class.

In short, Alban cheerfully received Amphibalus into his house, and gave him everything he needed, because even

17

though Alban didn't know Christ's Law, he still acted like a benign and virtuous prince.

Not long after, Alban looked for an opportunity to have a private conference with his visitor, and when they were alone together, he said, 'By many signs and tokens I can see that you are a Christian man: why have you put your body and your life in danger by coming among pagans? How are you going to get out of here without being killed?'

Amphibalus replied, 'By the grace of Jesus Christ, and by his mercy, if I have deserved it, I have been kept from danger, and dangerous places. Christ, God's son, has preserved my body. He has been my guide, and saved my life: he has brought me safely to this city to teach his glorious law and faith.'

'How can this be true?' asked Alban; 'I would very much like to learn who this is, this son of God – something new and strange! Did God have a son? Explain yourself!'

'I will, if you can listen patiently,' Amphibalus replied; 'I will spare nothing to tell you the truth, in detail.'

Reason persuaded Amphibalus to base his explanation on the Gospel, and to describe how our faith is recorded in holy writ. 'This is our belief,' he said; 'listen well. The Son, most perfect and most good, was incarnated and became flesh and blood, a man, like Adam the first man. And by His divine power, the Son was born of a pure woman, who had the perfection of virginity.

'The glad and gracious time of summer was approaching,' Amphibalus went on, 'when Queen Flora clothed the soil in a sweet tapestry of green mixed with every other colour, and the amorous spring, cherishing the sun and April's showers, brought in the flowers of May. The season was heavenly and divine: the winter storms had passed, and Phoebus shone through the rain. It was in this season, then, that a message was sent down from heaven, to say that, for the happiness of all mankind, a branch should spring out of Jesse.

'The news was sent to Nazareth, and the angel Gabriel was the messenger. By consent of the whole Trinity, the Holy Ghost came down in a straight line into the breast of a pure virgin. Luke, in his Gospel, tells us that Gabriel addressed Mary meekly, saying, *Hail Mary, full of grace, chosen by God above all others, the tabernacle of the Trinity, blessed among all women!*

'When she had heard the angel's words, Mary's chaste humility made her doubt what he had said, but, seeing that she was afraid, the angel said, *Oh Mary, don't be afraid of this! You have found grace before God. You shall conceive a child in your virginity, and he shall be born in Bethlehem, as the Gospel can bear witness, and when he is born you shall call him Jesus.*

'*How can this be?* asked the glorious maiden: *I have known no man either in will, deed or thought.* The angel replied, *As I said before, this miracle shall be performed by the Holy Ghost, and the virtue of God himself will alight in your breast. And the lord that shall be born of you, men shall call him the Son of God, as the prophets wrote long ago. Such heavenly grace has fallen upon you that you will stand above all women, and your light shall shine above the seven stars.*

'*May everything that you have said be fulfilled!* said Mary, with all humility, *behold this handmaid and humble servant!* Though God was pleased with her virginity, the scholars tell us that He was most pleased with her devout meekness.

'In this way a virgin, through her perfection, was made worthy to bear her Lord; a daughter was chosen because of her pure cleanness to bear her father, though she was still a virgin. Because of her unique merits, she alone among women was simultaneously a virgin, a mother and a wife. She was a virgin, to fulfil the will of God. She was a servant to the Lord because of her meekness, and also a daughter and a mother. When we remember this, we Christians bring a spiritual gladness to ourselves, and we also remember how this brings us safety, as predicted by the prophets.

'And so, dear host, believe my doctrine with your whole heart and it will stand you in good stead! God has sent me to teach you and to advise you, so that you will humbly desire to be His knight and do him reverence. I am here to tell you what will happen if you obey His Law and all his precepts.

'You will gain such power through faith in Him that you will be able to make blind people see, just by using the name of Jesus Christ. You will be able to rescue people from trouble, and heal lepers and lame people, and indeed cure all illnesses through the power of God. By God's providence, you will be able to escape all harm, live long, and avoid the plague, as long as you stick to God's Law. The Lord will not hesitate to grant your wishes, and at last, before you go from here, you will die by martyrdom.

'By martyrdom you will end your life, and then you will pass blissfully out of this world. In this way, you will escape all the trouble and transitory strife which menace you here day by day. Through Christ's power and grace you will go to God with patience and meekness. This is the reason for my coming here. I was sent by Jesus to this town, to act like a town crier, to bring you news of how you will patiently endure pain and passion for Christ's faith, as a knight and martyr, chosen for his service.

'That is His will, and this will reward you for the great

humanity and hospitality you have shown to people trapped by illness and poverty. You have performed seven deeds of mercy, which are already recorded in heaven: you have fed the hungry, visited prisoners, sheltered people who had nowhere to stay, helped the bed-ridden, comforted the sick (giving them everything they needed), and buried the dead.

'All the good things you have done are recorded for ever in the court of heaven. The Lord has remembered all your good deeds, so that he can reward you with the palm of victory, and let you reign with him for ever in paradise – a greater victory than the conquest of Troy!

'Because you have never hesitated to offer hospitality, and have never tired of feeding poor folks, and promoting the cause of the poor, God will not hesitate to pay you back, even though you live here as a pagan. If you continue to do all your good deeds after you are baptised, then you will be crowned with a double palm.'

Like a princely knight, Alban attended to everything that had been said, and asked, 'What type of worship shall I practice then, when I have turned away from idols, and turned to Christ?'

Amphibalus answered, 'You must believe wholeheartedly that there is only one God; the Father, Son and Holy Ghost joined in one. This is the foundation of our belief, as I will show you. If you humbly submit to believe in it, this faith will direct you clearly and help you avoid and correct all your old errors. I will go so far as to say that the beginning of your life has been acceptable to God, and your soul will be a great treasure for Him.

'The Father brings eternal power; the son brings great wisdom; and the Holy Ghost brings grace in particular, by virtuous providence. These three, which are called three in one, undivided: they never part; and if you long to turn to the Law of this great, imperial majesty, he shall make you live with him (this blessed lord, this blessed Trinity).

'Where He is, there is always joy and happiness: before his everlasting face the angels sing all together, *Hosanna*.

'Don't doubt any of this – set aside all hesitation – give up the company of your false idols – they are made of metal, and stone, and wood. Saturn, Jupiter, Mars, Apollo – they cannot help you, any more than those false goddesses, Diana and Juno! Though they have ears, they can't hear you; and their large eyes can't really see. They are just made of gold and stone – if you call to them, they can't help you.

'Now, dear host, forsake this crew, as I have said, and delight in Christ, and by His grace he will make you perfect.'

For a long time, Alban had listened closely and disdainfully, but now he shot up out of his seat and, as he went out, he began to say, 'You are not wise; your doctrine is hollow. If people knew you were here in this city, you'd have a very rough time indeed! All kinds of tortures would be brought out especially for your destruction. Your blasphemy would be punished unmercifully, and, at the end, your head would be struck off, if anybody else knew you were here. I fear for your safety – but I will advise you and protect you, so that no man will know about your thoughts and actions.' With that, Alban stormed out, looking very angry.

But Alban was not really angry: by the grace of God and by good fortune, everything he said, he said respectfully. His gentleness meant that he was never impatient, and he suffered everything with humility. Nevertheless, he could not fully accept the doctrine that Amphibalus had explained to him, and he couldn't decide what he should believe.

So when the moon was shining brightly, Alban found that he was so oppressed with tiredness that he decided he should get some sleep. But all that night, Amphibalus, by contrast, was on his knees, like God's own knight, praying for Alban.

God heard his prayer, and sent a dream to Alban as he slept. This dream was so elaborate and strange that Alban couldn't understand it at all.

In the morning, the sun shone brightly in the sky and Alban woke up out of his sleep. He was still puzzled and astonished by his strange new dream, and couldn't say anything about it. So he got out of bed and went straight to his friend, the pilgrim, to ask him what the dream meant.

'My friend,' he said, 'if everything you have told me about Christ and his Law is true, you must use your wits to interpret the strange dream I had last night. I'll try to tell you everything I can remember of it.

'It started with me looking up to a great house in heaven. Truly, I thought I saw a man come down out of that place, down to the earth. This man was so beautiful – I have never seen anything like him – but he was immediately surrounded by rude, noisy people.

'These people were bold and spiteful, and they tormented the man with whips, and made his sides bleed. Then they tied up his hands and nailed him to a cross: they gave his body four wounds with the nails they used to put him up, and one more wound with a spear.

'He was naked, and painfully stretched out on the cross, so that every nerve and vein in his body was snapped. When they pierced his side with a spear, it split open his heart. The wound was so deep that blood and water ran out.

23

'They also used a spear to give him a drink, but this was just a mixture of vinegar and bitter gall. Before, they had set a crown of thorns on his head, and they called him *King of the Jews*; but they called him this maliciously, out of spite.

'I thought it was terrible, what they did to him: they mocked him and said that if he was really the son of God, he should be able to come down from the cross unaided. It grieved my heart to see him so ripped up and tormented, with blood on his clothes. He was like a meek little lamb.

'After all these grievous and intolerable sufferings; all this hideous mortal torment, he cried out, *Into thy hands, father, I commend my spirit*, just as he was at the point of death. With that, he died.

'They took him down from the cross, and the blood flowed out of his fresh wounds like rivers. Then they sealed up his body under a great stone.

'He was closely guarded by knights in plate-armour and mail-coats, but they could do nothing to stop him rising up – their minds were overcome by sleep. And then I saw an angel, all clothed in white.

'The most amazing thing I saw in my dream was the man rising up out of his sealed tomb, like a strong champion. I saw and remembered the whole thing, in great detail.

'Forty days after this resurrection, the man ascended into heaven, conveyed by a multitude of angels, who sang more sweetly than any of our British singers!

'They looked so strange, the angels who revered him, all in clothes whiter than snow or milk. They sang *Blessed be the father, blessed must he be, and the son also blessed in his humanity!*

'This is the strange news I received in my sleep, and many

other things as well: secret things that I noted carefully; things that should not be described to any mortal man.'

This was what Alban told Amphibalus when he woke up, humbly begging him to explain it all. And Amphibalus was delighted to hear all this: he felt a spiritual gladness to see that God had come to Alban, and he began to fashion a cross.

'Here,' he said, 'is the sign, clear as the sun, of everything that was shown to you in your dream. The man you saw, sent from heaven, so beautiful and glorious, I tell you that that was my own Lord, Jesus Christ, who is most benign, meek and virtuous. He it was who suffered on the cross, as you saw in your vision. This he did graciously, to redeem all our sins, right back to the apple Adam ate in Paradise, because the serpent fooled him into it. Oh, that apple caused chaos for Adam, and his descendants, until Christ's passion – that was like a medicine for us.

'That serpent was mad at Adam, and his poison flowed out unabated, until Christ gave his blood on the cross. That blood was a balm, a medicine, like honey; the drink of all drinks, distilled by a miracle from Christ's five wounds – to bring life out of death!

'Christ's passion is our restorative – our health and our defence – that stills the boiling of our mortal strife. It is an imperial balm against the violence of the fiend. It is the quintessence of heavenly science, made to restore all mankind. It cures all sickness – even the sicknesses that the doctors give up on. It is our leech, our Hippocrates, our spiritual Galen, our Sampson that vanquished the lion, our mighty champion, the famous strong Achilles! Our hero bears up heaven for our salvation, high on the cross, ransoming us. He was the man you saw in your dream – the man who overcame Satan.'

'This is now my faith: this is what I believe,' said blessed Alban, with all humility. 'There is no God but my lord Jesus, who came down from his father's see to become humble and human, like us. He did this to help us, and bring us to salvation, to suffer for us through his mercy.'

Then Alban fell to his knees before the cross and repented, saying, 'Oh lord Jesus, have mercy on my misdeeds; receive my penance, you who bled on the cross for me.'

Inspired by grace, Alban strove to bind himself to Christ's Law, and at his baptism he said:

'I forsake the pomp of Satan and his barons, and all the power of the ugly fiends. I give my soul and body to Jesus, who died for mankind, and, as I believe, rose on the third day.'

Then Amphibalus said, 'Be strong in faith! Our Lord is strong in you. He will not fail to strengthen your heart by showing you his kindness. Others, before you, learned about Jesus from other men; but your dream-story shows that you have learned about Jesus by direct experience and revelation. He has declared everything to you directly: his birth, his passion, his resurrection. He has shown you these things directly, to call you to him as his chosen knight.

'I think that your vision means that now you can teach others about Jesus, without further help from me. And so I hope you will not be sad if I leave now. My conscience moves me to preach Christ's law in other countries. And they do say, don't they, that friends cannot always be together.'

'Friends can never be parted,' said Alban, 'if they are joined together by virtue and grace. Wherever they may be, such friends are always together in God. But please, don't leave so soon. Stay for a week, to teach me and make me perfect in Christ's doctrine.'

Amphibalus could not deny his request, and they spent the long night together in prayer. They hid away to do this, away from the noise of people, and spoke about Christ's Law the whole time.

But, out of envy and malice, a cursed pagan spied out the place, and went to the magistrate to accuse them both. He told the judge how they had met, and what they were doing, and this made the judge so mad, it was as if he was on fire!

The cry went out that Alban and Amphibalus should appear before the judge, and the town was ransacked, but they could not find them. Blessed Alban, moved in his heart to keep his master safe, had conveyed him out of the city at night. As they parted, both of them wept bitterly, and felt that they would die: their hearts were joined together in one chain until death.

Such love inspires the heart with boldness, and banishes fear. This was shown when Alban gave his gold-fringed cloak to Amphibalus, eagerly spreading it over his shoulders, just before the two friends parted. And so they said goodbye; but God had not forsaken them: he was their guide.

Instead of his gold cloak, Alban put on Amphibalus's old cloak, which was torn and threadbare. So, plain and poor-looking, with his mind set on Christ, he returned home.

And there he lived like a poor man, turning his back on wealth. He won his treasure by kneeling before the cross: that was his joy. And there I will leave him, praying, while I tell you how his enemies proceeded against him.

A new law was proclaimed in the town, saying that anyone who refused to kneel before the pagan gods, and throw incense in the fire for them, would be seized, tied to a pagan altar, and killed as a sacrifice.

This was a superstitious ceremony; a new thing that the pagans had introduced to combat the effect of Amphibalus's preaching in the town. And the magistrate was determined that Alban should be the first to suffer by it.

Alban knew all about this, but he was strong and steady in God, and ready for either life or death: whatever God chose for him.

When the summer flowers were at their best, blowing white and red, and Phoebus was making his journey from Cancer to Leo, the pagans of Verulamium, that royal town, took exception to Alban's conversion to Christ's faith.

They stood against him with such obstinacy that they were like wild boars or raging tigers. Their mad hearts were full of vengeance and fury, and their faces were grim and pale. All night they cursed Alban and Amphibalus with frightful words, menacing them like ravenous wolves.

Night's dark tides began to withdraw their shadows; the black skies flitted away, and Lucifer began to show his bright beams. Aurora forsook the fiery Titan's bed, and Phoebus' chariot began to light up the horizon.

A balmy wind began to blow through the meadows, and among the flowers and leaves, and a pearly, silver dew began to wet the soil. It seemed that Nature had ordained a fresh, bountiful day: that was the day when Alban's house was besieged.

Early in the morning, when the larks were saluting the new day, the pagans gathered in force to pursue Alban, the noble prince. They were planning to chase Amphibalus in particular, but he being gone, they fell upon Alban instead.

They found him kneeling before the cross, but he quickly

stood up when they entered. The judge had sent quite a multitude, and they fell on him like wolves, tearing at him.

They brought him before the judge, and there he stood, meek as a lamb, but ready to do battle like Christ's own knight. His banner, standard and sign were the cross of Christ, under which flag he was ready to either live or die; and with this sign lifted high in defiance of the pagans, he was ready to fight, like a champion.

God was with him to sustain his part, and he was steadfast of heart and hardy as a lion. He put his own life in jeopardy for Jesus, and though he was unarmed, Truth was his coat of mail, Faith was his shield and sword, and Hope was his spear and his pole-axe, stronger than steel. Armed like this, he was sure of victory.

He was cruelly dragged to the place where the pagans sacrificed to their idols, which Alban now despised. The judge, Asclepiodotus, was there, with the whole city. Alban, God's knight, stood among them, holding the cross that made him invincible. Although he and the pagans who surrounded him were of the same race, the heathens continued to curse and malign Alban. But when the judge looked upon the cross, he felt afraid.

The judge asked Alban where his master was. 'Where is this strange fellow, who despises our gods, and came here to deceive the city?'

Alban paused for a while before he replied, 'He has departed by God's order.'

The judge replied, 'Wherever he is, smuggled away or hidden, he has fled because of his faith. He could not stay here and stick to his doctrine; which shows that his preaching has no foundation! If his faith was firm,' the judge went on, 'he would have come here to me. But his heart is full of remorse. If his faith was constant, he would have acted like a good master, and stayed here with you, instead of leaving his disciple in danger. I think this man's doctrine is false and deceitful. His teaching is fraudulent, and it seems to have driven you mad. Why else would you give up your treasure and your riches, and turn your back on our gods? You are acting out of brazen wilfulness: you have become malicious and spiteful.

'Now you stand in great peril. That clerk has lured you into a snare, dislocated your reason and stripped you of your wits. Now you have taken up the cause of Christ, and declared war on all our gods. That is blasphemy, and it would be unjust of me not to exact the vengeance of the law on you. And the law says, blasphemers must die!

'You listened to a fool, and believed him, and his folly has seduced you. First, you do no reverence to the gods, and you will not be reconciled to them. You have crippled yourself – nobody will show you favour any more. You are vile and abject, compared to what you once were.

'But, any man may be taken in by such false, alien ideas. You can surely see where you've gone wrong: take my advice – forsake that sect, fall down and beg forgiveness, or you will suffer the full rigour of the law.

'If you ask for pardon, all your wealth will be returned to you. If you sacrifice to our gods, your wealth will even be increased, along with your reputation. You will be the lord of towns and castles: all you have to do is abandon Jesus.'

With heart and mind together, Alban stood his ground. The judge had both flattered him and threatened him, and also made alluring promises, but Alban stood firm and fearless in the midst of it all.

'Your menaces and your promises, your bold speech and your frowning face,' said Alban; 'these cannot move me. Jesus Christ is everything I need. I don't need to think about my decision: I despise your gold, your treasure and your gods.

'You have *accused* my master of treachery and duplicity; but be assured that God has *excused* him. What he did, he did by my advice. He didn't run away because he was afraid of you. I wanted him to leave; otherwise he would be here.

'I will not turn my back on the truth: everything you have said has been said in vain. I believe what my master taught me, and I will never turn away from faith in Christ: this is the faith that straightens the lame, and makes the blind see.

'This faith is firmly fixed in my mind, and it is more precious to me than all the gemstones that come out of India, or all the riches you have mentioned. Compared with faith, gold, treasure, pomp and pride are all transitory things.

'My faith makes me so strong and wealthy in myself that it has taught me to despise all worldly goods. I don't need to speak at length about this: I will not sacrifice to false gods, or worship them in any way. They are all hollow frauds: whoever worships them must be mad, or blind!

'These gods, with all their idolatry; they lead men astray: I've seen this in the lives of my friends, and my family. I defy those rascally gods! They have always been false and treacherous, and they still are today. They always betray their devotees!

'I will never have anything to do with them, and I certainly won't make a fire on one of their altars. This is my answer – note it well! And I won't put incense into their censers, or kneel before them – not in nine hundred years. That is my last word on the matter.'

At that, the people began to weep and cry out. They stood around the martyr, glaring at him like madmen. He heard them, and tolerated their violence and the menaces of the judge, but said nothing.

The people wanted their cruel vengeance, and they immediately dragged Alban to their temple. They tried to force him to sacrifice to their gods by lighting a candle to them. But Alban, God's knight, was strong and firm of heart, and he would never agree to make such a sacrifice.

So the people stripped him and scourged him, as Jesus had been scourged, until his skin was ripped to shreds. But he suffered all this gladly, lifting up his eyes and saying to God, 'Lord, guard my inmost thoughts: grant me patience in this time of pain. Do not let me bear a grudge against these people. Jesus, do not disdain my frail flesh. Don't let me grumble. My will is strong: I offer you my life and my soul!'

And so he continued to pray, all through his sufferings. He remained unbroken and unchanged, like a diamond. Neither cruelty nor the kind words of the pagans would sway him.

After this, Alban was put into the hands of the judge, like a lamb given up to the dogs, and was imprisoned for six weeks. During this time, nature began to complain about the way he was being treated, as if the earth were withdrawing its benefits from mankind. There was no dew seen in the mornings, on the soil, or on plants, grass or flowers. And there was no rain, or even a shower, to enrich the land. Flora, the queen of flowers, slept, and nobody felt any smooth, soft breezes.

By day, the earth was scalded by the furnace of the sun, and even at night, the heat was intolerable. The sky was so dead and grey that no fruit could grow, and no grain could be cultivated, so that it was useless to plough the uplands.

In this way, heaven and earth complained about the injuries done to God's knight.

The people themselves complained that there was no food to eat, believing that nature was fighting on Alban's side, and against his tormentors, because of sorcery.

The judge, Asclepiodotus, hated Alban, yet he could not kill him straight away: first, he had to send letters to the emperor Diocletian, explaining what Alban had done. He also had to wait for a reply from the emperor: because the emperor knew Alban, and also because of Alban's dignified position and his high birth, Asclepiodotus dared not proceed against him until he had authorisation from Rome.

At this time, the whole empire was employed in punishing rebels; particularly those who rebelled against the Roman gods. The emperor himself sent an army into Britain, led by Maximian, nick-named Hercules, to hunt down Christians and kill them all – except for Alban. He alone was to be spared, on condition that he turned away from Christ's Law, and returned to the law of the pagan gods.

So Alban was not only threatened every day – he was also forced to listen to arguments that were supposed to turn him away from his faith. His captors even repeated their promises of castles, towns and lands; but he would not change: he stood calm and firm between fire and water.

At last, Maximian determined that if Alban would not give in to either threats or promises, a knight of good reputation should be found to smite off his head. Only a well-respected knight could do this, because Alban was such an important man.

By contrast, it was decided that if Amphibalus was caught,

he should be tied to a stake, and a hole made at his navel. His bowels should then be pulled out through the hole, and wrapped round both himself and the stake. When he had died in this way, it was commanded that his head should then be struck off. This was the decision of Maximian, who was then with Asclepiodotus in Verulamium: both of them were quite mad.

The people came from far and wide to hear this judgement given in open audience: they even came from London, and many other towns. It was also decided that, after Alban had been beheaded, his head should be sewn back on, and his body sealed, together with his cross and his cloak, into a lead coffin. The coffin was then to be placed in a large tomb, which was to act as his monument.

The people were sad to see their noble lord in this plight, but when it became clear that he would not turn from Christ, and was determined to die, it was decided that Holmhurst should be his place of execution.

And so Alban was led through the town, like a lamb among the wolves, weighed down with chains. Devoid of pity, the people came out of the town to witness his martyrdom, as they would to see some uncouth spectacle. So many came that the judge was left alone in Verulamium. When they saw Alban, the people cried out, 'Drag our enemy out of the city! This is what happens to blasphemers! He's the cause of all our troubles!'

The numbers of people there increased all the time, so that soon there was nowhere for anybody to stand. They followed Alban, and soon they came to a deep river that menaced them with its sturdy waves. The bridge over the river was too narrow for so many people, and a number fell in and were drowned. Others swam across. Some made it onto the bridge, but the sun's heat was so merciless that they fainted and fell off.

When Alban saw all this mischief, he wept and fell to his knees. He prayed to God to staunch the flood and dry up the river, and that is what happened, straight away! His God was, after all, the same God who had defied Pharaoh and dried up the Red Sea, allowing the people of Israel to walk across without getting their feet wet.

Because of Alban's prayer, the river vanished, and its bed was suddenly dry and smooth. The drowned people who lay on the river-bed rose up, alive, and there was no sign of death on their faces.

Witnessing this, the knight who had led Alban out of the city, who was also the man detailed to behead him, was suddenly afraid. Inspired by God, the knight, who was called Araclius, threw away his sword, and knelt down before Alban. 'Servant of God: blessed Alban!' he said. 'I am sure your God is the only true God. The miracles I have just seen have convinced me! I beg for forgiveness for my past crimes, and cry to God for grace! There is no Lord but Jesus Christ, and I am now his knight!'

As soon as he had said this, the pagans fell on Araclius like spiteful wolves. They said that Alban's God had not dried up the river, but that their own sun-god Phoebus had done it, to allow them to cross over.

When they had said this, the people smashed the knight's teeth, and broke every one of his bones, so that every part of him was wounded. But his mind remained whole, and true to Christ.

As Araclius was lying, pale and half-dead, by the river, the pagans dragged Alban through sharp briars and over the stumps of many trees, to the place of his passion. The stumps, the briars, and the stones, which were as sharp as spears, meant that he left a trail of blood behind him, as they dragged him up the hill to his death. Truly, who could see a prince suffering like this, without shedding a tear?

At the top of the hill, where Alban was to fight his last battle, many people were waiting. The sun was so intolerably hot that the people were ready to die of thirst, but the heat merely drove them to be more cruel and spiteful.

Confronted by their hatred, Alban showed his love, and prayed for the people who tormented him. He prayed with his whole heart, and the tears ran from his eyes. He prayed that the people's fury would diminish, so that they would not suffer for their cruelty. He also prayed that a soft wind would cool the people off, and that a spring would appear to quench their thirst.

As Alban prayed, a flowing spring appeared, though the hill was dry and had had no moisture in it before. And so the people's thirst was quenched, and the air was cooled by a light breeze, but they were still determined to see Alban's death, and they claimed that Phoebus had made the spring for them.

They seized Alban's long hair and dragged him to the stake. Then they chose a knight and told him to be ready with his sword to behead Alban.

When he did so, the head remained in place: only the martyr's body fell. His cross was also sprinkled with blood, and this was kept as a relic. A Christian man was hiding in the crowd, and he took the cross without anyone noticing.

As for the knight who beheaded Alban, he was immediately blinded: his eyes fell right out of his head, and so he lost all his worldly joy forever. In this way, he was punished for wanting to see Alban bleed.

Meanwhile Araclius still lay wounded by the river. When he

was told that Alban had been killed, he rose up, wracked with pain, and began to crawl up the hill on his hands and knees.

Soon the judge appeared and said, 'I can see that you have many broken bones: climb up quickly and pray to your Alban. Cry out to him to heal your wounds. Run to him, and put his head back on his body: then you'll be cured, and you'll be able to build a tomb for him!'

The judge said all this maliciously, but the knight listened carefully to every word. 'I trust that God *will* restore me to health,' he said, 'because of the goodness of Alban.'

And so the knight crawled up the hill and found Alban's head. He embraced it, and wept over it, and soon he stood up, whole and sound!

He gave praise to God and to Jesus, and stretched himself out on the ground. He praised Alban too, in front of all the people.

Then he began to gather stones to make a tomb for Alban, laying them out in a row. In this way, he made a grave, and covered it over with fresh turf.

The pagans were shocked and offended by Araclius's cure, and thought it unnatural that a man so badly injured could be cured so quickly. They began to plot the knight's death among themselves, saying that he had been cured by witchcraft, or some experiment. They even suspected that Araclius might have taken a magic potion to make him impervious to daggers, swords and knives.

At last, a great many pagans fell on the knight, and cut off his head. Araclius was therefore able to be part of Alban's victory, and to share his reward with him.
When they had killed Araclius, the people went back to the city, singing a song about the victory of their god, Phoebus.

At night, Jesus caused a heavenly stream to come out of Alban's tomb. This was as bright as a sun-beam, and shot straight up into the sky. It shone all night, lighting up all four regions of Britain, but nobody knew what it meant.

The people of Verulamium came out of their city again, to examine this strange light with a mixture of joy and dread. They also heard a song coming out of the light; sung in Latin: 'Albanus vir egregius martir extat gloriosus'; and in the sky they saw and heard heavenly angels singing:

Let us with song upraise and magnify
The laud of Alban, notable and glorious,
This day with martyrs made victorious!

Bibliography

Bede: *The Ecclesiastical History of the English people*, Oxford, 1999

Eusebius: *A History of the Church from Christ to Constantine* (trans. G.A. Williamson), Penguin, 1989

Gildas: *On the Ruin of Britain* (trans. G.A. Giles), Dodo Press

Nennius: *The History of the Britons* (trans. J.A. Giles), Forgotten Books

Niblett, Rosalind: *Verulamium: The Roman City of St Albans*, The History Press, 2010

Paris, Matthew: *The Illustrated Chronicles of Matthew Paris*, Alan Sutton, 1993

Pearsall, Derek: *John Lydgate*, Routledge and Kegan Paul, 1967

Petts, David: *Christianity in Roman Britain*, Tempus, 2003

Renoir, Alain: *The Poetry of John Lydgate*, Routledge and Kegan Paul, 1967

Runcie, Robert (ed.): *Cathedral and City: St Albans Ancient and Modern*, Martyn, 1977

Salway, Peter: *A History of Roman Britain*, Oxford, 1993

Schirmer, Walter F: *John Lydgate: A Study in the Culture of the XVth century*, Methuen, 1961

Thomas, Charles: *Christianity in Roman Britain to AD 500*, Batsford, 1985

Webb, J.F. (trans.): *The Age of Bede*, Penguin, 1998

Webb, Simon: *In Search of Bede*, The Langley Press, 2010

Webb, Simon: *In Search of Saint Alban*, Langley Press, 2013

Webb, Simon: *Nicholas Breakspear: The Pope from England*, Langley Press, 2013